A Touch of His Love

Other Books in This Series

A Touch of His Love

MEDITATIONS ON KNOWING & RECEIVING
THE LOVE OF GOD
WITH ORIGINAL PHOTOGRAPHS BY

CHARLES STANLEY

ZondervanPublishingHouse
Grand Rapids, Michigan

A Division of HarperCollins*Publishers*

Requests for information should be addressed to:
Zondervan Publishing House
Grand Rapids, Michigan 49530

Library of Congress Cataloging-in-Publication Data

Stanley, Charles F.
    A touch of his love / by Charles Stanley.
       p.   cm.
    ISBN 0-310-54560-9 (hard)
     1. God—Love—Meditations. 2. God—Love—Worship and love—
Meditations. 3. Love—Religious aspects—Christianity.
4. Devotional calendars. I. Title.
BT140.S72   1994
231'.6—dc20   94-18293
                                             CIP

Edited by Gerard Terpstra
Cover design, interior design, and line illustrations by Art Jacobs

Printed in the United States of America

94 95 96 97 98 99 00 01 02/❖MV/10 9 8 7 6 5 4 3 2 1

This edition is printed on acid-free paper and meets the American National Standards Institute Z39.48 standard.

Contents

Photographs

Acknowledgments

To a highly valued member of our In Touch staff, Jim Daily, I express my deepest appreciation for his helpful editorial assistance for this volume.

And to Tim Olive, my photographer friend with whom I shared the unforgettable experience of shooting and printing these photographs, my sincere thanks.

Introduction

I was headed for burnout, but I didn't know why. I called together four of my friends and asked them to meet and pray with me. Thankfully, they did, and my time with them led me to a fresh discovery of God's love.

From that day on, I began to experience and "feel" God loving me; and it has never been the same. Since that moment, God, whom I had followed and obeyed all my life, became my Friend. I had new intimacy with the Savior; and I soon found that the more I loved him, the more I trusted him.

Knowing, receiving, and extending the love of God is the essence of the Christian faith. There is nothing more powerful, more encouraging, more settling, than embracing the love God has for you. God loves you as much today as he ever will, so you don't have to perform perfectly. He has pledged his unfailing love to you in every circumstance.

A Touch of His Love unveils the power and reality of the love of God. It is my prayer that Christ's unconditional love for you will saturate your mind and spirit and remove any false perceptions you may have about the character and ways of God.

The love of God is the big picture that puts everything else in right perspective. That was Jesus' emphasis when he said that the sum of Christian living is to love God enthusiastically and to love your neighbor as yourself (Matt. 23:37–39). That dispels petty rules and legalistic lifestyles that nullify the amazing grace and love of Christ.

My friend, whatever you face today, remember that Jesus is the same God "yesterday, today, and forever" (Heb. 13:8). That means that wherever you are and whatever you need, God loves you.

That is all you need to know.

A Touch of His Love

We know and rely on the love God has for us.

1 John 4:16

Experiencing God's Love

Something was missing. Somehow, after twenty years of ministry, I sensed I had an incomplete picture of and relationship with my Savior. I still preached every week. I continued to practice essential spiritual disciplines. However, something was definitely amiss in my own soul.

I became so restless and dissatisfied that I called four of my friends, all Christian counselors, and asked them to meet with me. It was on short notice, but amazingly, they all agreed. We sat down together on a Monday afternoon. Until late the next morning, they quizzed me, conversed with me, and endeavored to help me find the answers I was seeking.

I poured my heart out to God and these men, but there was still no release or rest in my spirit. As we were about to conclude, one of them said to me, "Charles, put your head on the table. Imagine that your father just picked you up in his arms. What do you feel?"

An emotional dam burst precisely at that moment. I wept for a long time. In fact, I had a difficult time stopping. I wasn't sure what God was doing, but he had obviously touched the most sensitive spiritual nerve of my soul.

When I settled down, the same person asked me how I felt. "I feel warm and secure and loved," I replied and immediately began weeping again. This time, however, I realized what God was doing.

I had trusted God since I was a small child. I had no trouble obeying him. I understood the importance of prayer and the priority of God's Word. What I never truly embraced or experienced, however, was the love of God. His sweetness and loving-kindness had somehow remained a footnote in my Christian walk. That is why I seldom preached any messages on the love of Christ. How could I preach what I had not personally experienced?

Through the godly help of my friends and the tender ministry of the Holy Spirit, I was able to identify the cause of that inner void. You see, my father died when I was an infant, and I simply didn't understand what the Father love of God was all about.

That encounter radically changed my life. Everything took on new purpose and meaning. My fellowship with God entered a new dimension. It was as if I started the Christian life all over again.

There may be something in your life that hinders you from fully experiencing and enjoying the most marvelous, liberating power in heaven and earth—the superabundant, absolutely transforming love of God. Quiet yourself before God for a season and ask him to make you newly aware of his love for you. Let him use whatever instrument he chooses and work in whatever way he determines.

Like me, you will begin a fantastic new adventure with God that sweeps away the dregs of the past and pours a fresh foundation for a vibrant, personal friendship with Jesus Christ, the lover of your soul.

God, help me to understand anew the vastness of your love. I know intellectually that you love me; but I want to experience it for myself, not simply read about it or examine it in a Bible study. Draw me into your love and keep me there.

TOUCHSTONE

*The adventure of God's love
never ends.*

As the Father has loved me, so have I loved you. Now remain in my love.

John 15:9

The Pattern of Love

While other religions of the world present strict and complicated teachings or devise complex philosophies, Christianity shouts that "God is love" (1 John 4:16). What a contrast and what relief!

But that should not surprise us, because throughout eternity, there has been a spectacular love relationship between the Father and his Son. Before the creation of the world and man, before time, Jehovah God and his only begotten Son lived in a perfect love relationship.

Although God loves man lavishly, he first bestows his perfect love on his Son, who in turn loves the Father joyously and unceasingly. And though there is no mention of the Father's love for the Holy Spirit, we know that the Trinity was and is ablaze with pure, unadulterated love, because the Spirit's desire is to glorify the Son.

After Jesus was baptized by John the Baptist, the Father in heaven expressed his delight with the Savior, announcing to all: "This is my Son, whom I love; with him I am well pleased" (Matt. 3:17). Jesus told the Jews that "the Father loves the Son and shows him all he does" (John 5:20). Speaking intimately to his disciples at the Passover Supper, Christ said plainly, "I love the Father . . ." (14:31).

Any attempt to coldly calculate the Trinity or to describe the ministry and relationship of the Father and the Son apart from divine love is not the true gospel; for every biblical principle, every utterance of Scripture is bathed in the love of God and the love of Christ.

Still more amazing is that the kind of love that exists between the Father and the Son can be experienced by you and me. Again teaching his hand-picked disciples at the Passover Feast, Jesus astounded them with these words: "As the Father has loved me, so have I loved you. Now remain in my love" (John 15:9).

The love of God the Father for his Son and the love of the Son for his Father are gladly dispensed to every Christian. God invites you through faith in his Son to share his love. His love has been deposited in your heart. Jesus cares for you with the same kind of love that the Father demonstrated to him. Can you imagine abiding, living, and resting in this incredible love?

Lord, today I especially need to sense your comforting love and protection. My days usher in new challenges at every corner, and it's during these moments that I need to experience your love and comfort. When I ponder the way you comforted your Son, Jesus Christ, as he faced death on a cross, I am strengthened and renewed for each day.

TOUCHSTONE

Jesus cares for you.

The LORD is close to the brokenhearted and saves those who are crushed in spirit.

Psalm 34:18

Of Reeds and Wicks

Have you ever tottered on the edge of despair, so disillusioned and disheartened that you wondered if God really loved you anymore? Have you been so wounded by painful circumstances or another's distressing actions that you questioned if God could really heal your hurt?

We all have experienced the anguish of such moments; and if our perspective on the love of Christ is clouded, we can succumb to spiraling depression and bitterness. How grateful I am that our Savior comes to our aid at such times with tender love.

In describing the nature of the coming Messiah's ministry, the prophet Isaiah said, "He will not shout or cry out, or raise his voice in the streets. A bruised reed he will not break, and a smoldering wick he will not snuff out" (Isa. 42:2–3).

More than eight hundred years later, Matthew thought of Isaiah's words and used them to describe Jesus' earthly life as he healed broken bodies and relieved tormented minds, touching the lives of physically and emotionally damaged people. Some were blind and mute, even demon-possessed. Most, no doubt, were social outcasts. But Jesus, with exquisitely sensitive compassion, changed their dreary, desperate world into one of renewed hope and confidence. And the One who does not change is poised to illumine darkness with the radiant light of his love.

If you feel like a "bruised reed" about to break or a "smoldering wick," your soul exhausted and almost extinguished, take courage. The love of God is both strong and tender enough to heal your hurts and revive your spirit. At your weakest moment, God's love is completely sufficient to sustain you.

You can count on God's tender mercy to rescue and restore you in your darkest hours. The Great Physician quietly comes into your pain and goes about doing what he does best—touching, healing, restoring men and women who are weary. He never snuffs out the slightest plea for hope, the parched cry for relief and help. Just call on him. He's already there, with healing in his wings, eager to impart strength for the journey.

That's good news, isn't it?

Lord, I am hurting right now, to the point of numbness. The only comfort I truly have at this moment is knowing that you are gently holding me in your arms. It makes me realize that you have always been faithful to get me through the storms. This gives me the confidence and comfort to carry on.

TOUCHSTONE

*Jesus' tender love is the
rainbow at the end
of a storm.*

We meditate on your unfailing love.

Psalm 48:9

Unfailing Love

If there is one topic that I delight in meditating upon repeatedly, it is the object of the psalmist's contemplation—the unfailing love of God. Nothing so comforts me, so steadies me, so nourishes me as the truth of God's unfailing love for his people.

The writers of the Old Testament used the rich Hebrew word *hesed* to express this characteristic of God's care. It is sometimes translated "loving-kindness" or "steadfast love." It incorporates the staggering reality that God's love simply cannot let his people go.

Flowing unceasingly from the heart of God is love that will never let you down, never disappoint you, never forsake you, never fail you. The writer of Hebrews said it this way: "Never will I leave you; never will I forsake you" (Heb. 13:5).

The steadfast love of God never changes, is never diminished by my behavior, is never quenched by my indifference or even rebellion. The loyal, covenant-keeping love of Christ is ever fresh, ever healing, ever faithful, ever sufficient.

Since God's love for you is unfailing and unchanging, you need not be unsettled. "For the king trusts in the LORD; through the unfailing love of the Most High he will not be shaken" (Ps. 21:7). Those were the words of David, whose life was constantly in peril. His safety and stability rested securely in God's remarkable love for him, and so do yours.

I would like to suggest a spiritual exercise that I believe can revolutionize your knowledge of God and your relationship with him. The concept is expressed in the oldest psalm of the Bible, penned by Moses: "Satisfy us in the morning with your unfailing love, that we may sing for joy and be glad all our days" (Ps. 90:14).

Each morning, think upon God's unfailing love, how it is expressed to you, its immensity, its power, its nature. Let God satisfy you with the sure knowledge that he has set his love upon you and will never turn it away. The more frequently you ponder God's boundless love, the more joyful you will become. The more joyful you are, the more exciting is your walk with Jesus and the more dynamic is your faith.

The unfailing, steadfast love of Christ for you is your anchor for every storm, sustaining you, keeping you, upholding you. It satisfies the deepest longing of your heart.

Heavenly Father, I can hardly imagine what your unfailing, unceasing love really means. I do know that it is what I yearn for in my heart. Each day, grant me a more complete understanding of how much you really love me. Along the way, teach me how to express that love to those around me. Thank you for creating the need for love within me and supplying that need. Amen.

TOUCHSTONE

The love of God will never let you down.

For great is his love toward us.

Psalm 117:2

Receiving God's Love

One of the first verses of Scripture I learned as a young Christian (and probably the verse most believers can quote from memory) is John 3:16: "For God so loved the world that he gave his one and only Son, that whoever believes in him shall not perish but have eternal life."

As I have grown in Christ, I understand that the entire Bible, every verse, is the revelation of God's love for mankind. From Genesis to Revelation, it is the story of Christ's unflagging desire to redeem and reconcile human beings to an eternal fellowship with himself.

How then did I develop such stubborn resistance to receiving and enjoying God's love? Why are so many other Christians caught in the same spiritual snarl that ties up our fellowship with God and dangerously entangles our whole viewpoint of the Christian life? We know that God is love, but our knowledge of his love runs only skin deep. We know much about sound doctrine, but our soul is starved for the love of God.

There are some basic factors involved. Perhaps the most obvious is pride, the taproot of sin. It is a devilish snare that promotes the deceptive thinking that once God has rescued us from eternal ruin, we can make it on our own. It binds us in an exhausting, exacting lifestyle that rarely displays Christ's character and seldom satisfies us. Pride repels the love of God. It breeds self-reliance, short- circuiting our need for love.

Yet beyond pride, I feel there is still a rather common malady that kept me and prevents others from even having a clue of what Christ meant when he said, "Now remain in my love" (John 15:9). Jesus used the Greek word *agape*. This word was seldom used by the Greeks and had little cultural weight, but Jesus and the writers of the New Testament injected it with supernatural significance, using it to express the unconditional love of God for the believer.

Unconditional love means this—God loves you just the way you are. Isn't that something we all ache for, to be loved without conditions or stipulations? God loves you when you obey, and he loves you when you err. That doesn't mean he tolerates sin—he died for it—or that he dilutes its consequences. But it does mean that his love for you is amazingly steadfast and unchanging.

Perhaps it is because the concept is so alien that we know embarrassingly little about God's agape love. But that can change today. God loves you as much now as he ever will. God's love is freely bestowed on you by his choice. It may sound too good to be true, but it is God's idea. Receive it, accept it, and you will never be the same.

Heavenly Father, I did not realize that pride can take root so subtly. I am probably unknowingly struggling with its snare. Expose those areas where its roots are cutting off complete devotion to you. As I humble myself, reveal your words of love throughout Scripture so I may be solidly grounded in an understanding of agape love.

TOUCHSTONE

*For God so loved me, he gave
his Son so I can have
eternal life.*

We have peace with God through our Lord Jesus Christ, through whom we have gained access by faith into this grace in which we now stand.

Romans 5:1–2

The Cure of Grace

I admit I have a "type-A" personality. I like well-defined goals. I enjoy accomplishment. I want to do things better. There is nothing inherently wrong with this mind-set, but it can lead to a biblically deficient lifestyle that defuses the awesome power of God's grace.

The gospel is the good news of God's grace. Jesus was full of "grace and truth" (John 1:14). The message of the apostles was the triumph of grace over law. Apart from the cornerstone of grace, the gospel would be fundamentally flawed. You cannot understand Christianity or the love of Christ until you major on grace.

Grace is God's kindness and graciousness toward humanity without regard to the worth or merit of those who receive it and in spite of the fact that they don't deserve it. God's grace toward the believer means that we cannot do anything to make God love us any less or any more. Think on that!

What this does (to type-A personalities like me, as well as to every other human disposition) is dismantle the tiresome treadmill of performance. I don't have to be successful to be loved. I don't have to fulfill certain obligations to be loved. I am loved by the God of all grace because there is nothing I can do to earn or merit his love.

What a wreckage this makes of our traditional thinking. But that is precisely what grace does. It goes against our grain because it flows from the fountain of God's supernatural love. We don't have to do anything to merit God's pleasure; we already are pleasing to him once we receive Christ's forgiveness of sin.

If that sounds radical, you're right. Grace says, "You can't— I can." It says, "You've failed. That's okay. I will help you. I will restore you." You can do nothing to earn salvation because it is a gift of God's grace. And you can do nothing to merit his continued favor, for, as Paul says, it is grace "in which we now stand."

Are you working hard to gain God's favor? You have it. Is there always something more you think you have to do in order to be accepted? God has done all you need through the cross of Christ to make you acceptable.

We are saved by grace through faith (Eph. 2:8). We live to the praise of his grace (1:6) and are enjoined to be strong in the grace of God (2 Tim. 2:1). Christ's performance on the cross has been credited to your account so you can be free to live life "to the full" (John 10:10). It is a sufficient promise.

Lord, I've been plagued with feelings of guilt lately, believing I wasn't doing enough to earn your fellowship. But Romans 5 tells me I already have peace with you because of your grace. I don't have to do or be anything! Jesus Christ did it all. I want to spend the next few moments thanking you and meditating on the reality of being totally accepted by you—just as I am.

TOUCHSTONE

You cannot do anything
today to make God love
you any more or any less.

This is love: not that we loved God, but that he loved us and sent his Son as an atoning sacrifice for our sins.

1 John 4:10

Supreme Love

Do you ever question God's love for you? Do you sometimes feel as if you have somehow wandered outside the sphere of his compassion into a bewildering state of turmoil and problems?

When such disconcerting thoughts and feelings disturb you— as they do most of us—there is a remedy that can keep you from stumbling into despair and discouragement. The cure for this sentiment is the cross of Jesus Christ. Whatever doubts you may entertain about God's love for you can be instantly dispelled when you consider the anguish and benefits of Christ's crucifixion.

Jesus' brutal death on a Roman cross is the highest expression of God's love for man. Seated in divine royalty in the heavenlies, Jesus was sent to earth by the Father to execute his eternal plan for man's redemption. When you think of Jesus impaled on coarse timbers, hanging, hurting, bleeding, you are pondering the greatest act of love ever displayed.

For it was on the killing field of Golgotha that the sinless One took on our sins, incurring the holy fury of the Father against iniquity so we might inherit the glory of eternal life. Jesus died for you. He suffered for your sin. And wonder of wonders, he did this while mankind was still in rebellion against him. "But God demonstrates his own love for us in this: While we were still sinners, Christ died for us" (Rom. 5:8).

As he always does, God took the initiative to save mankind from sin and death. He made the first move by eliminating the obstacle of unforgiven sin through his all-sufficient, sacrificial, atoning death. Christ on the cross says "I love you" in the most endearing way possible.

Never doubt the love of God for you. Turn your focus on Christ's substitutionary death on your behalf. Think upon what he did for you and what he is willing to do today. For if "he . . . did not spare his own Son, but gave him up for us all—how will he not also, along with him, graciously give us all things?" (Rom. 8:32). The love that sent Jesus to die your death lives in you to provide for every need in every circumstance. It is undying love that will never let you down. That is the truth, the truth that will set you free.

Jesus, thank you for showing your utmost love by dying on a cross for me. When I doubt that you care, refocus my attention on Calvary. It is the eternal proof of your love.

TOUCHSTONE

The cross is the proof
of God's love.

But love your enemies, do good to them.

Luke 6:35

Defusing Hostility

It is a hard moment to forget. I had just become senior pastor at First Baptist Church of Atlanta after a time of controversy. As I stood in the pulpit at a meeting, one of the men approached me and struck me. That was only one of many incidents where the displeasure and anger of others were displayed.

Did I have a hard time dealing with my emotions? You bet. Did Jesus' command to love my enemies seem an impossible command? Certainly. But I discovered, and so can you, that the love of Christ can override our emotions and prime our will to obey.

David's awkward relationship with King Saul helped me learn how to treat those who hurt or mistreat me. Thoroughly misunderstood and relentlessly pursued, David spent years in crags and caves while Saul enjoyed all the perks of kingship. Twice, David had golden opportunities to slay his tormentor. David, however, refused to exercise that option of hate, choosing instead to demonstrate his innocence and loyalty.

David did not retaliate. If we are wise, we will travel the same route. Anytime we seek revenge, subtly or blatantly, we foil the power of God's love. Retaliation takes the matter out of God's providential hand and puts it in our sinful grasp. It violates God's law of love, which Peter defines this way: "Do not repay evil with evil or insult with insult, but with blessing" (1 Peter 3:9).

How do you not return the blow you've received? By taking refuge in the sovereignty of God. Jesus, when hanging on a cross, "did not retaliate; when he suffered, he made no threats. Instead, he entrusted himself to him who judges justly" (1 Peter 2:23). Both David and the Messiah made God their hiding place from the schemes of wicked men, trusting him to handle their hurts.

Better yet, entrusting yourself and your particular circumstance to God frees you to extend grace to the offending party. Love flowed from the cross. David spoke graciously and courteously to Saul, keeping hate at bay. Do good to those who wrong you. Speak kindly to them, and the gripping thoughts of retaliation will eventually slacken.

The noblest expression of love is to give it to those who don't deserve it. That is what Jesus did when he gave himself up for us, and aren't we called to be like him? Love your enemy, and your faith will never seem more real. You can do it because God is in control.

Lord, I readily admit my difficulty in holding my temper at bay whenever I am wronged by others. The need to "get even" can become so overwhelming, I sometimes feel out of control. Fill my thoughts with your words of love spoken to others. Whenever I see others who have offended me, prompt my spirit to speak kindly to them. I can do this only through the strength of your Holy Spirit.

TOUCHSTONE

Before expressing anger, ask yourself, "What would Jesus do?"

Man looks at the outward appearance, but the LORD looks at the heart.

1 Samuel 16:7

The Big Picture

Great Bible characters weren't always so great. Moses and Peter had very inauspicious beginnings. David encountered serious obstacles, some of his own making, throughout his life. Gideon started slowly, fared well for a season, and ended with some question marks.

That's significant to me and to you because it reveals some crucial facts about the Christian life that affect our ability to personally embrace God's love.

It tells us that God is as interested in the process as he is in the result. Those who trust in Christ as Savior will arrive safely in heaven. Jesus' performance on the cross settles that issue. This means that the process of becoming like Christ is what God is primarily up to in our short span on earth. This involves failure and success, joy and grief, wisdom and foolishness, peace and turmoil. Certainly, if you were to chart the lives of Moses and David, the graph would resemble a mountain-range silhouette. God wants you to exhibit and express the life of Christ, and that is a lifelong process.

It also tells us that God is concerned with progress, not perfectionism. The men and women that God used in Scripture and the people he uses today are far from faultless. What God does care about is a heart that is bent toward obedience to him, repentant when wrong, contrite when disobedient, humbled when overreliant on self. Progress includes failure, but it moves toward a growing relationship with the Savior. God put up with David's antics because the rudder of David's heart was set toward him. Probably what impresses and encourages me the most when I think about these men is this—God saw their huge potential for godliness and waited patiently for it to develop. What farmer discards a half-grown crop? He waters, watches, and protects it until harvest. When God saves you, he knows your tremendous spiritual potential. Peter's initial vacillations paled in comparison to his later loyalty and commitment. Moses' forty years of exile were but preparation for forty years of tough leadership.

If you know God is interested in the process, looks for ultimate progress, and sees unlimited potential, you can be liberated to walk and act under the umbrella of his love. God's commitment is for eternity, but he is with you today to help you make the most of each opportunity. If you falter or fail, he will correct you and help you walk upright again. When you look at life from this perspective, it encourages you to continue the journey and keeps your blunders under the overview of unconditional love and unending grace.

Gracious Father, I am so grateful that you see my life as one big picture with one magnificent plan. As much as I don't like valley experiences, it helps to know that you have not given up on me. I don't have to feel good only on the mountain tops. You are so good. I just want to thank you, Lord, for having the big picture in mind.

TOUCHSTONE

Today— it doesn't have to be perfect. Just keep the big picture in mind.

Though your sins are like scarlet, they shall be as white as snow; though they are red as crimson, they shall be like wool.

Isaiah 1:18

Red and White

While working in my photographic dark room one day, I made an interesting discovery, casting the prophet Isaiah's description of sin in a revealing light. I occasionally use colored filters over my lenses when I photograph in black and white. For instance, a light yellow filter darkens the sky, while brightening the clouds. A red filter enhances the white still more. That particular day, I experimented with viewing a red dot on white paper through a red filter. To my amazement, the dot, when seen through the red filter, appeared white.

At that moment I realized the overwhelming truth of God's forgiveness. Our sin, depicted as deep red by Isaiah, becomes white as snow and wool when seen through the red cross of Golgotha. This is the great transformation of forgiveness. Jesus, the Lamb of God, took away our iniquity when his blood was shed on the cross. Our past sins, today's transgressions, and tomorrow's disobedience have been fully forgiven by Christ's once-and-for-all sacrifice. By his own doing, God in Christ has cleansed you from every stain of sin. Though you still suffer damaging consequences when you sin, you are never treated as a sinner by the Father. You are a new creation in Christ, a saint, a holy one born of God.

God's forgiveness not only takes your sins away but also credits the righteousness of Christ to your account. This is a dynamic aspect of forgiveness that is often overlooked. No blame can ever be laid to your account, because you have been justified, declared "not guilty" by the Judge himself.

God is free to express the wonder of his love to you. There is no barrier, no hindrance, for the justice of God has been satisfied. Forgiveness pulls the plug on guilt. If you are fully and freely forgiven, why put yourself on an unnecessary guilt trip? The Holy Spirit will indeed convict you of sin, but you will never stand guilty before God.

This is how God sees you—pure as snow, white as wool. Your sins have been permanently cleansed through the shed blood of Christ. Since this is how he views you, shouldn't you see yourself in the same light?

Father, I get overwhelmed whenever I discover your truths being reinforced through simple objects and events. I can witness miracles and your promises being fulfilled by simply opening my eyes to your creation every day. Knowing that you see me as pure, whole, and blameless seems a miracle in itself. I want to thank you and praise you for your perfect, living example of love.

TOUCHSTONE

See yourself as God does.

My times are in your hands.

Psalm 31:15

Let It Go

Do you sometimes wrestle with God over an issue you desperately want solved? The need is urgent, the time is short, your prayers are intense. However, God seems tight-lipped. At times, there appears to be an almost inverse relationship between the magnitude of the problem and the clarity of the response from God. The more we want to know God's mind, the less he appears to reveal a solution.

After several such episodes in my life, I came to understand a potent scriptural truth that can unleash the full weight of God's power on one's behalf. Its dynamic meaning became clear only after I had come to the end of my resources. It is the principle of relinquishment.

When I reach my wit's end, when I have prayed as precisely as I know how, followed all the commands I know to obey, sought as much counsel as I thought necessary, and still have no clear guidance, I realize I must relinquish the entire situation to the Father. Never have I experienced such peace and such profoundly supernatural answers as when I relinquish the problem to God.

By relinquishment, I do not mean resignation or passivity. I am not suggesting a mind-set that centers on inaction. What I do mean is the cessation of a demanding spirit, the quieting of inner strife, the cancellation of my own agenda, and a complete willingness to settle for God's provision.

Christ himself is our example as he passionately communed with the Father regarding his death. "My Father, if it is possible, may this cup be taken from me. Yet not as I will, but as you will" (Matt. 26:39). Jesus knew his mission of redemption was incomplete without the cross, yet he still had to surrender his desires to the Father. It was a prayer of relinquishment, arrived at only after ardent, earnest petition. But what power flowed from the answer

—the cross of Christ, the crux of Christianity. Jesus, as always, said yes to the Father, and the shackles of sin were shattered.

The same principle releases God's amazing answers today. We submit to the Father's plan, whatever that may be. We give the matter over to the love of God and trust him for results that we may or may not like. Whatever the answer, it is from God; and that is all we need to know.

Relinquishing a troublesome matter to God means we have placed the dilemma squarely into the hands of God, whose goodness, wisdom, and power never fail. They are good hands.

Dear heavenly Father, I do have worrisome matters that plague me. I have tried to manipulate my circumstances, control others, and bargain with you. It has all been frivolous. Right now I want to give my circumstances to you. With open hands, I lay them before you, not holding on to any part of them. By faith, I am trusting you completely with my needs.

TOUCHSTONE

*You can let go of your
problem because God
doesn't let go of you.*

*Being confident of this, that he who began a good work in you
will carry it on to completion until the day of Christ Jesus.*

Philippians 1:6

No Complaints

Some of my fondest memories of childhood are of my mother. My father died when I was nine months old, so my mom supported the two of us for many years. She worked the swing shift at a textile mill, coming home late each night. We didn't have very many worldly possessions. In fact, we moved frequently, living in seventeen houses over a period of sixteen years.

Yet my mother seldom complained. She always expressed confidence in God to meet our needs, and she spread cheer wherever she went. Her enthusiasm and faith were contagious.

I can't help but think of her every time I read an engaging verse of Scripture tucked away in the second chapter of Philippians: "Do everything without complaining or arguing" (Phil. 2:14).

In seven concise, potent words, Paul unveils the lifestyle that repels bitterness, regret, and anger and promotes love. To be honest, I sometimes wonder how we can obey that command when confronted with situations that seem primed to bring out the worst in us.

Yet when I think of my mother and the many difficult situations she faced without a hint of murmuring, I believe I now understand her secret to a contented, thankful heart. It is not a secret really, for it is a principle that every believer can practice successfully.

It is found in the verse immediately preceding Paul's command to tackle life with a hearty spirit: "For it is God who works in you to will and to act according to his good purpose" (Phil. 2:13).

We must never lose sight of the tremendous truth that God is constantly and positively at work in each detail of our lives. He is never limited by circumstances, never perplexed over problems. He is actively moving in our inner being to conform us to Christ's image and is sovereignly steering events toward our good and his praise.

We can genuinely give thanks in everything (1 Thess. 5:16), because God is at work in all things. Why grumble or complain if God is in control and accomplishing his purposes? I am convinced that it was because my mother understood this principle that she was enabled to go about her duties with a grateful heart.

Do you see God at work in you? If so, then each assignment of the day, great or small, bears his imprint. Refuse to yield to a critical or complaining spirit because to do so is to actually grumble against God himself (Ex. 16:8).

A thankful spirit promotes peace and health. It acknowledges God's love and affirms your trust in him. And it is a solid testimony to others that the God you serve is able, caring, and very wise.

God, forgive me for grumbling and complaining about so many things. There is much to be thankful for. I know a grateful heart promotes peace, and that is what I want. I give you permission to change my critical spirit and replace it with thanksgiving.

TOUCHSTONE

Complaining is to the devil
what praise is to God.

Come to me, all you who are weary and burdened, and I will give you rest.

Matthew 11:28

Cease Striving

It was 2:20 A.M. I suddenly awakened from a restful sleep, sensing God had something to say to me. In a matter of seconds, Psalm 46 came to mind. I turned on the light and began to read. Although I am very familiar with this magnificent, comforting psalm, I read it deliberately and prayerfully.

The tenth verse arrested my soul: "Be still and know that I am God." In the quiet of the night, I knew God was revealing something that I desperately needed to know. I prayed, asking God to open up the meaning of the verse so that I might receive his fullness, and then I returned to bed.

The next morning I met with a group of pastors. As we prayed together, I shared my experience with one. He opened his Bible and read Psalm 46:10 from another translation (NASB): "Cease striving and know that I am God."

As soon as I heard the words "cease striving," I knew what God was saying to me. Though I know better, I have a tendency to strive in my own strength and energy. Let me tell you, that's exhausting, frustrating, and ultimately not very productive in God's scheme. As long as you think you have to perform a certain way to please God, you are in subtle conflict with him.

I breathed a sigh of spiritual relief as I saw the futility of my attempts to carry out God's commands with my resources and his amazing adequacy for every demand. I can "cease striving" to be holy and righteous, because "in Christ" I already am holy and righteous. I don't have to strain to gain God's approval, because he already loves me unconditionally.

Do you see how this removes the struggle? Do you understand how this can help you to relax and rest in the all-sufficiency of God's grace? Christ, who indwells you through the Holy Spirit, is your peace, strength, comfort, wisdom, hope, joy, and guide. You have all this because you have Christ.

You work diligently "with all his energy which so powerfully works in [you]" (Col. 1:29). You plan wisely, but with the knowledge that God's will is preeminent (Prov. 16:9). You pray fervently, but with the knowledge that God's response is always best (Jer. 33:3).

We "cease striving" when we "know that [he is] God." We don't have to white-knuckle it through life, because our sovereign God is in control. We don't have to bend beneath life's emotional load, because our loving God invites us to cast our cares on him. We don't have to manipulate our circumstances, because our wise God has a good and kind plan. We don't have to yield to our weaknesses, because our omnipotent God strengthens us for every trial and temptation.

God, I relinquish _____ to you. I have tried to solve the problem my way and find myself exhausted. I will accept your solution and cease striving for my own. You know this matter has greatly troubled me. It is not easy to give it over to you. But I choose to let it go and cast my burden on you.

TOUCHSTONE

*God has provided everything
I need through Christ
and his work on the cross.*

Yet I hold this against you: You have forsaken your first love.
Revelation 2:4

The Priority
of Relationship

Are you as much in love with Jesus as you were when you first met him? That is the kind of question that can take your breath away, isn't it? It cuts to the core of the Christian life. Is your relationship with Jesus your priority, or have you become immersed in superficial service that has all the trappings of Christianity without the thrill and vitality of personal fellowship?

If you have a nagging sense that your fellowship with Christ has slowly cooled and dropped to lukewarm, then you need to consider these questions: Is Jesus still "your first love"? Does God still excite you? Is time spent in Scripture rewarding? Is telling others about the Savior fascinating? Do you begrudge giving God a tithe of your income? Your responses reveal much about the quality of your relationship with Jesus. Knowing him as your first love means you are increasingly excited about his character, his ways, and his Word.

Activity, though essential to practical faith, is not a substitute for personal fellowship. It can never outweigh intimacy with God. Our relationship with Christ erodes and cools when our primary focus is taken off the Messiah and placed on other things. That is the beginning of idolatry, and it is a dangerous path for the saint to tread. The gods of this age—sports, work, money—are cleverly disguised and ensnare many Christians with their compelling allegiance. Too much of a good thing can be wrong if it distracts you from devotion to Christ.

How can you recapture that first love? Remember what Christ did for you when you were saved, the supernatural transformation that took you from death to life, from darkness to light, from the dominion of sin to the reign of Christ. Repent of whatever has dampened your love for Jesus. Turn away from all that distracts you. Spend time in prayer and study with the single purpose of encountering God—listening, worshiping, obeying.

As a young Christian I was introduced to the writings of Oswald Chambers, who put one's relationship with Christ above all else. In his book *The Moral Foundations of Life*, Chambers wrote, "Never allow anything to fuss your relationship to Jesus Christ, neither Christian work, nor Christian blessing, nor Christian anything. Jesus Christ first, second, and third, and God himself by the great indwelling power of the Spirit within will meet the strenuous effort on your part and slowly and surely you will form the mind of Christ and become one with him as he was one with the Father."

How easy it is, Lord, to drift in my relationship with you. I'm not sure how I got to this point of mediocrity, but I want to return to you, my first love. Take away whatever has diluted my fellowship with you. May you truly be "first, second, and third" in my life. Refocus the gaze of my soul that I may see you at work in all things.

TOUCHSTONE

*First love gives God
first place.*

[Paul] traveled through that area, speaking many words of encouragement to the people.

Acts 20:2

An Encouraging Word

The words are still hung and framed neatly and permanently. Not on my wall, but in my mind. They were spoken when I was only six years old. One memorable day, as I was leaving my school room, I overheard my teacher comment to another, "I like Charles." It was the first time a person other than my mom had ever said she liked me. I was elated. Her three simple words were high-octane emotional fuel that boosted my confidence and even changed the way I viewed myself.

Have you ever thought how influential the words you speak are? Do you know what kind of impact your speech can have on a person who desperately needs to hear an encouraging word? Solomon wrote, "Pleasant words are a honeycomb, sweet to the soul and healing to the bones" (Prov. 16:24). What a wonderful way to describe our conversation. It can be medicine to a weary soul, healing to a bruised spirit. Kind words, spoken in due season, are God's bridges of love.

If you've been on the receiving end of gracious comments, you know the power of well-chosen words. Perhaps a coach noticed you at practice one day and remarked how well you had performed. Or maybe a co-worker came to you and commended your work and attitude on a difficult task. Paul describes such speech as "full of grace, seasoned with salt" (Col. 4:6). Our remarks, he says, are to be flavored with gentleness and loving-kindness, key ingredients of grace-filled speech.

The love of Christ can leap into the hearts of others through your words when you speak to them the way you want them to speak to you. Let words of cheer and praise be the order of the day, and you'll be amazed how you can change the atmosphere of your home or office. The golden rule is never more effective than when it regulates our speech.

Ask God to make you aware of the needs of others. When we are completely absorbed in our problems or activities, complimentary words rarely grace our conversation. Accept others the way they are and allow God to change them through his Spirit. Your focus is on edification, not condemnation. Your speech is targeted for "building others up according to their needs, that it may benefit those who listen" (Eph. 4:29).

Let your tongue be God's instrument of love. Speak words that young girls and boys and men and women in your neighborhood, your office, your home, your church, your school can't wait to hear.

Heavenly Father, speak through me words of encouragement and cheer. Make me sensitive to the needs of others around me, while taking my eyes off of self.

TOUCHSTONE

Speak to others the way you
want someone to speak
to you!

May the Lord direct your hearts into God's love.

2 Thessalonians 3:5

Lovers of God

Jesus had many harsh words for the religious Jews of his day. Members of groups like the Pharisees and Sadducees relied on peer-pleasing appearances and culturally accepted norms of behavior for their approval. They were like many individuals today who conform to external standards of religion but lack any vital union with the person of Christ.

Jesus Christ described such men with one sweeping but profound statement when he addressed a proud, belligerent crowd in Jerusalem: "I know you. I know that you do not have the love of God in your hearts" (John 5:42). Their formality, their desire to please men rather than God was but a visible symptom of a basic spiritual deficiency—they did not love God nor hold him in awe in their hearts.

How would you describe yourself as a Christian? Are you a follower of Christ? Are you someone who obeys the Scripture? While these certainly are solid working definitions of a believer, would you call yourself a lover of God? When you love God rightly and sincerely, it is amazing how everything else in the Christian life fits.

The Jews had a myriad of laws and regulations that governed their distant, cold knowledge of God. Jesus shattered that legalistic maze when he said that the two greatest commandments are that we love God with all our heart and our neighbor as ourselves (Mark 12:30–31). The accumulation of thousands of years of lifeless laws was, in a matter of seconds, reduced to the essence of Christianity. Jesus knew that when a person loves God, he doesn't waste his time worshiping insignificant and trivial pursuits. He understood that a person who loves his neighbor won't murder, steal, engage in adultery, or fabricate lies. Loving God and others fulfills the law.

If you are a lover of God, you seek intimate fellowship with him. You covet his approval, while accepting the acknowledgment of others with humility. A lover of God seeks to know him, accepting his blessings simply as gracious gifts. A lover of God reads and studies the Scripture to encounter Christ personally.

Saint Augustine penned this intriguing thought: "Love God and do as you please." That sounds irresponsible at first glance, doesn't it? However, think about it, and you will agree that the person who truly loves God will act out of a heart that delights in pleasing the Father.

Are you a lover of God? If so, then you are a man or woman after God's own heart.

Lord, I do love you. I may not know exactly how to express my love, but I know I can count on you to instruct me through your Word. I ask you, Lord, that you will supernaturally empower me to love others as Christ loves them. Guard my intentions, that they will not be misunderstood. Let others see Jesus, not me.

TOUCHSTONE

*Love God, and you will do
what pleases him.*

Let us . . . love with actions and in truth.

1 John 3:18

Love in Action

He was my Sunday school teacher, and a good one. But I remember him for something else. Craig Stowe would stop me on the street while I was on my paper route and purchase a newspaper. He would spend five or ten minutes chatting, asking me about my family, school, and things that matter to a young boy. Not only that, he always gave me more than what the newspaper cost. It didn't take me long to figure out that Craig Stowe didn't need to buy a newspaper . . . he got the newspaper at home.

What that man did each week for several years demonstrated God's love to me. He went out of his way to show that he wasn't just my Sunday school teacher. He involved himself in my life in a tangible fashion, and I will never forget him.

Kind words are gentle healers, but kind deeds are megadoses of the love of Christ. Jesus didn't just say he loved us; he demonstrated his love by dying for us (Rom. 5:8). Only hours before he was to die, Jesus told his disciples that the world would know they were his followers by their love for each other (John 13:35). He obviously meant they would have a lifestyle that visibly and practically expressed God's love.

Barnabas became involved with a discouraged young man named Mark, who later penned one of the gospels. Mary and Martha showed their love for Christ by inviting him to dine and rest in their home in Bethany. Paul reminded Titus that Christ's death not only saved us from sin but should be the motivation for us to be "eager to do what is good" (Titus 2:14). We are even "created in Christ Jesus to do good works" (Eph. 2:10).

So go ahead and bake that pie for the mom who just arrived home from the hospital. Mow that yard for the elderly man whose arthritis has almost immobilized him. Invite that lonely person from the Sunday school class out to lunch. Take time for a coffee break with that frustrated co-worker. Help the new neighbor unload the boxes that are still in his garage. Write that encouraging note to the young man or woman who is struggling to adapt to the college routine.

Sharing God's love in this manner incarnates the compassion of Christ and says "I care" louder than any words possibly could. All it takes is a willing spirit to lift another believer. Nothing but good comes from doing good.

Lord, I've been a little slothful with my idle time lately. I worry about my own problems so much that I forget that others around me have needs as well. Show me how to demonstrate your concern to others around me. Thank you for the memories of times when others have gone out of their way to show me special attention. These memories have always been a boost when I've been down.

TOUCHSTONE

Actions say more than you think.

I will . . . praise your name for your love and your faithfulness.
Psalm 138:2

When We Praise

The more you love God, the more you will worship him. Love and praise are natural partners. Heaven is a place where those who love God live in constant praise of him. Should your present experience be any different?

We praise God for what he has done. "Praise him for his acts of power," writes the enthusiastic psalmist in Psalm 150:2. His "acts of power" are the extraordinary events recorded in Scripture—creation, miracles, the cross, the resurrection. They also are the remarkable displays of his personal love for you. Why not write down some of the ways that God has demonstrated his power in your life? Think of his guidance, his provision, his protection, and the numerous other ways he has supplied your personal needs. A journal that records God's handiwork in your life is a tremendous launching pad for joyful praise.

We praise God for "his surpassing greatness" (Ps. 150:2). This is pure praise, standing in awe of God for who he is. He is faithful. He is kind. He is good. He is just. He is holy. He is patient. He is generous. God acts greatly because he is a great God. His character and attributes should overwhelm us. Our response should be nothing short of ecstatic gratitude. Think of this: you have the opportunity to praise a personal, perfect God who takes great interest in who you are and what you do.

Praise magnifies God and puts problems into perspective. What obstacle is too big for God? What circumstance is too perplexing for him? Many times I have come to God with a consuming burden, only to find it light and easy after a session of praise and worship.

Praise reveals our devotion to Christ. Habakkuk the prophet wrote that he would praise God even in the worst of times, when the "olive crop fails and the fields produce no food, though there are no sheep in the pen and no cattle in the stalls" (Hab. 3:17).

Even if you are caught in such a worst-case scenario, God still deserves your praise. And from experience, I can tell you that praise is the one factor that will deliver you from the sinkhole of depression and discouragement.

Express your love for Christ by putting a priority on praise. Make it a point to enter his presence with a thankful heart before you present your requests. Choose to praise in difficult straits. It makes all the difference, because it focuses on the God who makes the difference.

O heavenly Father, I do want to simply praise you. I do not want to dwell on any of my problems or needs, but only on all you've done for me. Your Word tells me that from the very beginning of time, you had me in mind, desiring all the while for me to accept your Son as my Savior. You have watched over me, orchestrating my life for my good and your glory. Thank you for all you've done for me.

TOUCHSTONE

Praise fuels love's engine.

No one can snatch them out of my hand.

John 10:28

That Loving Feeling

Sir Winston Churchill once remarked that it was dangerous to "always [be] feeling one's pulse and taking one's temperature." His words were addressed to those who looked at the wildly fluctuating fortunes of battle to determine England's success or failure in World War II.

His words are apropos as well for the Christian who constantly gauges his relationship with Christ based on feelings. Emotions are unreliable barometers, and if you attach your faith to them, you are in for an upsetting experience. Certainly, we are to love God and do those things that please him, such as reading his Word, spending time in prayer, and joining with a local body of believers. But there are occasions when the Bible seems cold, our prayers listless, our commitment to the church uncertain; and if we allow our feelings to govern our fellowship with Christ in these instances, we are sure to drift into self-condemning, guilt-ridden waters.

The crux of the matter is not relying on your degree of love for God for stability and security. This is much like holding the proverbial wrong end of the stick. The prescription to a steady, progressive walk of faith is focusing on God's love for you. His love is unchanging and fixed forever.

Think about this illustration: Imagine your hand and God's clasped together. Your grip loosens during a season of temptation, sin, doubt, or apathy. Your feelings of love for God are minimal. But rather than concentrating on your slackness, look to the hand of God. His grip of love is solid. He will not let go. "Your right hand upholds me," declared David in the forlorn deserts of Judah (Ps. 63:8). "For I am the LORD, your God, who takes hold of your right hand," said God to a fearful people (Isa. 41:13).

You are eternally secure in the love of God. You are sealed by the Holy Spirit with the unperturbed life of Christ. Heaven is reserved for you. In this light, you can cease, as Churchill said, from the paralysis of morbid introspection. You can stop depending on your irregular spiritual pulse as an indicator of your love relationship with Christ.

The favorable winds of God's love for you blow continuously. Move forward in that truth, and the turbulence of gusty emotions will not blow you off your course of growing in the grace and knowledge of Jesus Christ.

I can be so easily influenced by my feelings, and the results of my actions can be so devastating, Lord. Strengthen my faith walk with you. My heart's desire is to grasp your hand firmly at all times. Teach me to overcome feelings that are damaging to our relationship. Thank you, Father, for your steadfast love.

TOUCHSTONE

*Nothing can loosen God's
grip on you.*

For God loves a cheerful giver.

2 Corinthians 9:7

To Give

When I consider a scriptural synonym for *love,* I am drawn to the constant biblical use of the word *give.* "For God so loved the world that he *gave* his one and only Son . . ." (John 3:16). "I live by faith in the Son of God, who loved me and *gave* himself for me" (Gal. 2:20).

God gives you the gift of salvation and the Holy Spirit. He gives peace, strength, and wisdom to those who ask.

It is impossible to love someone without giving. We bestow our affection on family members and friends with various forms of giving. We demonstrate our commitment to Christ and others by giving our time, our resources, our energies. Generosity is the hallmark of genuine Christianity. "A generous man will prosper; he who refreshes others will himself be refreshed" (Prov. 11:25). Giving is the channel through which the love of God flows.

"But I have so little to give," you lament. That may be true, but as long as you wait until you have a surplus to give, you will never begin. A generous person primes the pump by giving even the little things—a listening ear, a tip for the grocery boy, a handmade gift for Christmas.

A generous person is happy. Others are drawn to a generous person, not for a handout, but because of the inviting spiritual atmosphere that surrounds him. A generous person is sensitive to the needs of others and gives genuinely, not for the purpose of manipulation. He receives joy in seeing others benefit from his benevolence. He views needs as an opportunity, not a threat. He wants to see how much he can give, not how little. He trusts God for his own needs.

Why is giving so important? Because it is the sure cure for greed, the antithesis of generosity. God blesses generosity and curses greed. Giving is the antidote for selfishness, a lifestyle that cannot reflect the likeness of the indwelling Christ.

Generosity opens the heart of both giver and recipient to the lavish love of Christ. Both can become spiritually wealthy and prosperous, enjoying the riches of the Christ-centered life. If you are reluctant to give, stingy with your resources, and isolated from the needs of others, you're missing out on fantastic blessings from your generous heavenly Father. "Give and it will be given to you," Jesus promised (Luke 6:38). Such is the power of generosity. It is the right choice to make. Give something today and watch God work.

Jesus, the first step is the hardest to take. Giving any amount or any thing appears sacrificial at this point. But I've read these words and I've listened to the testimonies of others that reveal the blessings that come from heartfelt giving. Today, show me a way in which I may give of myself to benefit others and glorify you.

TOUCHSTONE

*It's impossible to love
without giving.*

For Christ's love compels us.

2 Corinthians 5:14

Fish and Sheep

Peter had fished all night and came away empty-handed. It was now early morning, and the rhythmic lapping of waves against his boat made Peter all the more drowsy. Yet the intriguing words of Jesus as he taught from Peter's boat kept him awake.

"When [Jesus] had finished speaking, he said to Simon, 'Put out into deep water, and let down the nets for a catch'" (Luke 5:4). There is reluctance and weariness in Peter's response: "Master, we've worked hard all night, but because you say so, I will let down the nets." We know the rest of the story. The catch of Peter's life nearly took the boat down, and Peter learned an unforgettable lesson in obedience.

However, there was more to discover. Later Jesus, in his resurrected body, is again on the shore by the sea. Peter, sharing a meal with his risen Lord, is confronted by Christ: "Simon son of John, do you truly love me more than these?" (John 21:15). The question befuddles Peter. "Of course, you know that I love you Jesus," he replies. Twice more, Jesus queries Peter about his love for the Messiah. Peter reaffirms his commitment each time and finally receives this command from the Savior: "Feed my sheep" (v. 17).

This dramatic postresurrection dialogue with the Lord underscored a new beginning for Peter. The rough-hewn fisherman would no longer obey just because Jesus told him what to do, as in the Sea of Galilee encounter (Luke 5:5). He would not adhere to Jesus' words only because he was the Master, the Savior, the Lord.

Something greater was at stake. Peter's obedience, his future evangelization of other lands, and his leadership in the Judean church were to be motivated by love for Christ. Our obedience validates our love, but our discipleship is always prompted by devoted love for the Savior. Obedience that issues forth from love is a delight, not a burden; and it is the pure wellspring of the abundant life.

Do you obey God from duty or fear, or do you follow and serve Christ out of a heart filled with love? When the love of Christ "compels you," you are on the right road to godliness. Your relationship to Christ is the priority, and obedience is merely the follow-through.

Peter needed to reexamine his motivation for obedience. Jesus asked tough questions to prepare Peter for tough times. He will sift you as well if you allow him to, so that your obedience will spring from love.

Dear God, I know I've been doing things lately out of duty, not out of love. I do love you, Lord, and I want to please you, not out of fear of rejection, but out of love and devotion. Help me to discern the difference so I may be used effectively by you.

TOUCHSTONE

*The springs of obedience have
their fountainhead
in love.*

For great is your love toward me.

Psalm 86:13

Just for You

Our culture continues to grow increasingly impersonal. Perhaps, like me, you've been shopping in a large store and found it almost impossible to locate someone to assist you. The notion of personalized service in any sector is virtually archaic. And have you noticed how people are treated in generalities, classified by income level or categorized into a particular age group?

This kind of depersonalization bothers me. That's why it thrills me to know that God loves me as an individual. He does not think of me or you in generic terms, but has specific thoughts toward us as unique persons.

Jesus came to Bethany to resurrect Lazarus. Mary and Martha had earlier sent word to the Messiah about their brother: "Lord, the one you love is sick" (John 11:3). Lazarus was not just another person among the multitudes to Christ. He was a man whom Christ loved as a friend. Later, as Jesus approached Lazarus's tomb, he was moved to tears. "See how he loved him!" marveled those assembled nearby (v. 36).

Jesus loves you just as personally. He is interested in you, your hobbies, your vocation, your emotions, your needs. He knows you as distinct from all others. "You know when I sit and when I rise; you perceive my thoughts from afar. . . . You are familiar with all my ways" (Ps. 139:2–3). God's intimate acquaintance with David, all of his ways and quirks, moved David to amazement. We should be no less staggered.

Biblical expressions like "the apple of your eye" and "engraved on the palm of your hand" are God's ways of describing his incredibly personal affection for you (Ps. 17:8; Isa. 49:16).

Such love means that the Father has a plan for you that no one else can fulfill. Although his ultimate goal of conforming you to Christ's image remains constant, he has custom-designed events, circumstances, and relationships that will lead you into his will. He works in your inner being and in the routine of your life in a divinely original manner. He knows exactly what you need, when you need it. He knows your frame—how much pressure you can stand, your personality makeup, the composition of your soul.

Since God deals with you as an individual, your personal thoughts, words, and actions are of great importance, for you matter to God. You are uppermost on God's mind today. Isn't that fantastic!

It's good to know I have such an intimate Friend as you, Jesus. Because of your omnipotence, I can trust you to lead me through the dark shadows of life. I know you will always be right beside me. And because you are omniscient, you are aware of my innermost feelings better than I usually am. Thank you, dear Friend.

TOUCHSTONE

*God has a job for me that no
one else is qualified for.*

There is no fear in love. But perfect love drives out fear.

1 John 4:18

Banish Fear

Faith in God is frequently presented as the corrective for fear. There is no doubt that even a small dose of trust can move great mountains of phobias and anxiety. That is why I find the apostle John's prescription so fascinating. Love, John says, is the way to banish fear. In a strict sense, John speaks about love removing the fear of punishment, the fear of offending an angry God. But it is just as applicable to the entire emotional spectrum of fears and worries that trouble us. The Amplified Version gives the expanded meaning: "Full-grown (complete, perfect) love turns fear out of doors and expels every trace of terror."

John does not exclude faith as an ally when dealing with fear, but he stresses that love is an even greater spiritual weapon. Having faced many fears of my own, I understand his rationale. When we are afraid, faith seems distant. Fear wreaks such havoc with our emotions that trust seems unobtainable, unreachable. We want to have faith, but we appear quite faithless. Yet when we think of God's love for us in frightening times, great peace and comfort settle within. When we think of God's care for us, his absolute commitment to our entire well-being, "every trace of terror" can be exiled.

Perfect love is God's provision. Jesus said, "My grace is sufficient" (2 Cor. 12:9). The love of Christ is enough to conquer the source of any fear. Are you afraid of failure? God's love never fails. Are you afraid of the future? God's love has already provided for your tomorrows.

Perfect love is God's protection. You are held steadfast by God. He is a sure refuge and fortress to those who turn to him. God, who never slumbers, is the keeper of your soul. He is a sovereign hedge about you, allowing only those things to touch you that are first filtered through his love.

Perfect love is God's presence. God is with you in every situation. He abides in you so you can face each fear in the confident awareness that Jesus is Immanuel—God with us, and therefore God with you.

As you learn more about God's provision, protection, and presence, fear dissipates. His perfect love enfolds and encompasses you. The better you grasp his love, the easier it becomes to trust him. Kick fear "out of doors" where it belongs and replace it with the certainty that your loving God is taking perfect care of you.

> *The LORD is my shepherd, I shall not be in want. . . . Even though I walk through the valley of the shadow of death, I will fear no evil, for you are with me; your rod and your staff, they comfort me. . . . Surely goodness and love will follow me all the days of my life, and I will dwell in the house of the LORD forever. (Psalm 23)*

TOUCHSTONE

God's love is never-ending,
his protection ever-present.

Those whom I love I rebuke and discipline.

Revelation 3:19

Tough Love

God's love is not all fuzzy and warm. If that were true, then we must conclude that it is defective. A father and mother who love their son or daughter invoke disciplinary measures when necessary. Our heavenly Father, likewise, does not hesitate to correct us with loving discipline when our behavior violates his good and gracious ways.

David met the stern love of God on several occasions for his waywardness. The psalmist learned that God wasn't all sweetness. Peter felt the sting of God's tough love as he denied Christ. Paul had harsh words for Mark after the young disciple went AWOL on his first missionary journey. Eventually, we all discover that God is serious about the business of holiness; and when hard actions are called for, he will oblige.

Perhaps you have enforced strict guidelines with a strong-willed child. Or you have had to make some tough decisions at work regarding problem employees. Whatever the circumstance, love sometimes must be expressed in stern tones to be effective.

God's discipline, however, is always motivated by love. "The Lord disciplines those he loves" (Heb. 12:6). Don't fall into a pity party when God orchestrates his correction. It is actually a reminder that he cares for you enough to keep you from self-destructing. The unbeliever is still under God's condemnation, but the Christian is never condemned, only disciplined. That is good news.

The context of God's redress is a Father/child relationship. "Endure hardship as discipline; God is treating you as sons" (Heb. 12:7). You are not a stranger, an alien to God. You are his child and, as such, you experience his fatherly correction. Do not mistake his discipline as anger and feel that your relationship with him has cruelly changed. That is Satan's lie. You have been adopted into his family, and his discipline only enables you to fully enjoy the benefits of his fatherhood.

Never forget that "God disciplines us for our good, that we may share in his holiness" (Heb. 12:10). The pain of chastisement has a purpose—to help us live more like God himself. The dross of impure motives and dubious behavior is purged by God's tough love. It is cleansing, refining, and restoring.

Do not turn away or become bitter when God's sternness is directed toward you. It is a sign of his love, and the goal is to remove unnecessary baggage and to strengthen you for the journey.

My loving Father, I know I have done things in my life that have made me seem unlovely. I can recall paying the consequences for those actions, too. I realize now that you were in it all the while, and your loving hand of discipline kept me safe from myself and matured me in my walk with you. As much as I don't like to be disciplined, I am very grateful that you love me enough to intervene in my life in such a way. Amen.

TOUCHSTONE

*God's tough love comes from
a tender heart.*

He has given us his very great and precious promises.

2 Peter 1:4

Standing
on a Promise

At a crucial time in my life, when the church I pastored faced an overwhelming obstacle, God riveted my faith on this verse of Scripture: "You are the God who performs miracles; you display your power among the peoples" (Ps. 77:14). I meditated on that verse daily, applying it to the problem at hand. I wasn't sure of the outcome, but I was sure of the promise. Amazingly, God intervened and blessed the congregation with a supernatural answer.

You too can rely on the promises of God's Word. The Bible is a book of promises as well as principles. It is freighted with sparkling verses that declare God's intention to graciously bestow good gifts. Some promises are conditional; God will act in a certain way if you obey certain criteria, as in "Give, and it will be given to you" (Luke 6:38). But there are thousands of Scriptures that wait only for a ready faith and a willing spirit to claim them.

Bible promises are assertions of God's love for you. God has assumed full responsibility for meeting your needs and provides nourishing promises as one means of his supply. Claim a promise from God that applies to your particular need. If anxiety has become a part of your lifestyle, Philippians 4:6–7 and Psalm 46:10 are God's answers. You can be certain that God will fulfill his promise when the context of Scripture is not violated, when the answer to the promise glorifies God and demonstrates his character, and when the Holy Spirit quietly impresses on your heart that he is speaking to you through the specific promise.

As God's promise percolates in your heart, be patient. God operates according to his time schedule, not yours. He sees the end from the beginning and knows precisely when to act. Don't lose heart or be discouraged in the process. It may take days, months, even years for the promise to ripen, but God will keep his word. Remain focused on the promise, digesting its full meaning, letting God speak all he wants through the Scriptures. Be obedient in the daily rounds, yielded and submitted to the revealed will of God.

God's promises are anchors for your soul. They keep you grounded in his love and faithfulness, reminding you of your dependence on him. What God promises, he will fulfill. As David Livingstone, the noted missionary, said, "It is the word of a Gentleman of the most sacred and strictest honour, and there's an end on it!" Claim it as your own, and stand in faith until God replies.

Thank you, Lord, for standing behind your promises. They are reliable and trustworthy and for me. Your word is truth and I can always count on that when the need is great. Help me to learn your promises that apply to my circumstances and firmly bank on their fulfillment.

TOUCHSTONE

God doesn't break his promises.

So Jacob served seven years to get Rachel, but they seemed like only a few days to him because of his love for her.

Genesis 29:20

Time Flies

It can take an entire day for me to capture the image I want for a photograph. Waiting for the right amount of light, framing the shot exactly, and taking advantage of other nuances demand time. But those outings seldom seem long or tedious to me because I love photography. Time flies when you are having fun—when you love what you are doing and are excited about the results.

Do you love what you do or do you complain? Is your heart merry, having the continual feast of happiness that Proverbs describes (Prov. 15:15), or is it weighed down with anxiety or boredom? Regardless of the dullness or monotony of your surroundings, I am convinced that God can transform your attitude so you can approach your tasks and relationships with a cheerful disposition.

Jim Elliot, the missionary who was later martyred, said, "Wherever you are, be all there." You may want to be in another job, another marriage, another state, another home; but the key to enjoying life is contentment with your present lot, as difficult as that may be. The grass of another job that looks green to you now looked brown to the person who left it. Godliness accompanied by contentment is a "great gain" (1 Tim. 6:6). It's fine to dream and set goals, but focus your energy on making the most of where God has put you.

Learn to view your situation from this divine perspective: "That everyone may eat and drink, and find satisfaction in all his toil—this is the gift of God" (Eccl. 3:13). Your life is a gift from God, along with all that comes with it. Even in strenuous seasons, we can discover God's merriment. When you walk up that unchanging assembly line each day or walk into the office of that perpetually irritable boss, think of your circumstances as God's gift. They may not always be wrapped in pretty packages, but the events of your life are orchestrated by the loving hand of God for your good. The joy of the Lord really can become your strength.

A proven curative for transcending the mundane to taste of God's goodness is the knowledge that God rewards your labor. Our sins have been judged; so when we stand before our Savior and Judge, we will be rewarded for our labor (2 Cor. 5:10). Every day, every action, every moment counts for eternity, for God sees your heart and motives and will recompense you.

You can learn to love what you do, to enjoy being where you are, and to be satisfied with your relationships. When that happens—and it will if you integrate these principles into your thinking—then, as with Jacob, the years will seem like only a few days, and your joy will be full.

Abba Father, you know I have been unhappy in my current situation. I've been guilty of looking at others' lives, wanting what they have, not what I have. I want to make a change . . . right now. I need your help in changing my attitude. Instill in me a happy, cheerful outlook in all that I do, understanding that this is your will for my life.

TOUCHSTONE

*The only change you may
need to make in your life
is a change in attitude.*

God our Savior ... wants all men to be saved and to come to a knowledge of the truth.

1 Timothy 2:3–4

Evangelism Made Easy

Just talk about evangelism, and most people quiver. They know they haven't been to the latest soul-winning course, and they have difficulty communicating the gospel to their family, and even more to a stranger or a friend. The thought of visiting a home and fumbling through a verbal outline brings on the spiritual shakes.

I have some good news about sharing the Good News. It doesn't require any theological training. There's nothing to memorize, and you don't have to set aside a specific night of the week to make it work. Basically, I want to take away all the excuses and focus your attention on the simple truth that love is the greatest apologetic. More people are brought into God's kingdom through a Christian's love than through any other means. Jesus said others would know about our faith and Savior when we major on love.

People in your circles of concern—family, friends, neighbors, co-workers, social acquaintances—need Christ. God has placed you in proximity to their lives to help them know the love that God has for them. It doesn't have to be strained or forced. Their turning to Christ can happen spontaneously or progressively when you are God's vessel of love to them.

Begin by accepting them as they are. They may be rowdy, uncouth, immoral, or unethical. These are natural turnoffs to the Christian, but God wants you to love them despite their actions. You cannot expect regenerate behavior from an unregenerate person. You obviously don't have to agree with their lifestyle; but by accepting the person as someone special to God, you are demonstrating the completely supernatural quality of unconditional love. Remember the darkness you once lived in before salvation and how God's love drew you into his light.

Trust in the power of the Holy Spirit to save them. You don't have to know the right words. You don't have to have a stack of special evangelism-oriented verses. God will work through your ordinary ways to express his extraordinary love. The Holy Spirit is the only person who can regenerate an unbeliever. That is his job, not yours. Your words and deeds of kindness to the non-Christian build bridges for the Holy Spirit to work. He wants them saved more than you do.

Persevere. An unbeliever can build up some sturdy walls of reasoning to ward off the gospel. It usually takes time for God's truth to triumph. But there is no wall that God's love cannot surmount, no barrier it cannot penetrate. Extend the love of God persistently to those around you, and you will never think of evangelism as hard again.

Lord, when I think back, I remember that it was the demonstration of your love through someone else that made me yearn for you. I want to make that same impact on others I come into contact with. Keep my spirit sensitive to those around me and to their needs. Help me to be a light on their pathway.

TOUCHSTONE

*The Holy Spirit just wants us
to be there—he will do
the rest.*

Be kind and compassionate to one another, . . . just as in Christ God forgave you.

Ephesians 4:32

Righting Wrongs

It was a memorable dinner—not for the food, but for the conversation. In the dining room of our home, God was righting some wrongs between my children and me. I wanted to know if there was any unforgiveness in their hearts toward me or if while rearing them I had done something that deeply hurt them.

Andy spoke first, "Dad, do you remember the time you were in your study and I was practicing some music? I had played the same part several times, and you came into the living room and said, 'Andy, is that all you know?' As far as I was concerned, you were rejecting both me and my music. That hurt." Becky jumped in, "When I was five years old and we lived in Miami, you sent me to my room and made me stay there. I cried and cried."

Those were just the first shots fired over the bow. They shared other instances when I had offended them. Now, I could have defended myself, but I knew there was only one thing I should do—ask them to forgive me. They did, and the air of resentment and bitterness was cleared.

Whether you have wronged a person or a person has wronged you, forgiveness is the only viable option to fully experience the love of God. When you seek forgiveness or extend it, you launch Christlike love into the heart of the problem. An unforgiving spirit is poison. It stagnates Christian growth, pollutes your relationship with Jesus, and robs you of personal joy. A forgiving spirit hurdles emotional barriers and heals spiritual scars.

Start the healing process by first examining yourself and repenting of an unforgiving spirit. Thomas à Kempis wrote, "We carefully count others' offenses against us, but we rarely consider what others may suffer because of us." Continue the healing process by canceling the debt of wrongs against you. The process is emotionally charged, but it is a matter of choice, not feelings. This releases the person from your judgment just as God released you from sin's debt when he forgave you. Recognize that the offender has exposed an unforgiving bent in you that God can heal when you choose to pardon.

All time spent in the backwash of an unforgiving spirit is wasted time. It counts for nothing, advances nothing. But the moment you forgive, the restoration process begins. Bitterness loses its hostile grip, and the freedom of forgiveness is ushered in. You can never be fully free until you fully forgive.

Lord, it's incredible how past unresolved hurts can affect so much of our lives. I do not want anything to come between me and the love you have to give. I know there are hurts I must deal with and correct. Please bring to my mind those past wrongs and give me the wisdom to make them right.

TOUCHSTONE

It's never wrong to do right.

I love the LORD, for he heard my voice; he heard my cry for mercy. Because he turned his ear to me I will call on him as long as I live.

Psalm 116:1–2

Solving Problems Through Prayer

Two things are said to be certain—death and taxes. Let me add a third—problems. But unlike the first two, you can do something about the latter. You can pray. In his love, God has provided prayer as a means to forge fellowship with himself and provide access to his wisdom for our problems. God is in the problem-solving business, and when you present your dilemmas to him, he will answer. His reply may not be what you thought or wanted, and it may not fit neatly into your schedule. Nonetheless, God has entered into a covenant relationship with you whereby he assumes the awesome responsibility to help you, lead you, correct you, and make his will known to you. Prayer is the frontier of discovery.

Present your problem to God. Don't dance around what is bothering you. "God, you know the boy next door who plays the drums at midnight is annoying me and disturbing my family. Show me how to solve the problem without losing my temper." The more specific you are in prayer, the more readily you can discern his answer.

Expect God to act. God told his people to call on him and watch him do great things (Jer. 33:3). Your petitions are meaningless if you don't anticipate God's response. That is what faith is about—seeing him moving and working behind everything. Wait for the Lord's reply and remember that your problem awaits his solutions, not yours. In his essay "The Efficacy of Prayer," C. S. Lewis wrote, "If an infinitely wise Being listens to the requests of finite and foolish creatures, of course he will sometimes grant and sometimes refuse them." God's solutions are always best, even if they do not align with our desires.

Thank God during the interval. Thanksgiving acknowledges God's faithfulness and love when circumstances say otherwise. A thankful heart rejoices in the God who answers, as much as it does in the answer itself.

God is greater than your problem and is eminently able to resolve it. The power of prayer can never be overestimated because of the omnipotent God who hears and answers. Be willing to work out your difficulty his way, follow his instructions, and assume the risk that he may or may not remove the problem. In any case, your petitions will set the stage for the best possible solution, for you have put your trust in the God who cares.

How foolish it is of me, Father, to think I can out-think, out-plan, and out-solve an omnipotent, omniscient, omnipresent God. You know my tomorrows as well as you know my yesterdays. You know my needs before I do; and what's greatest is that you know the solutions.

TOUCHSTONE

No problem is too big for God.

For our light and momentary troubles are achieving for us an eternal glory that far outweighs them all.

2 Corinthians 4:17

Why, Lord?

"If God is all-powerful and all-loving, why do I suffer?"
This universal question has spanned the centuries, perplexing some, discouraging others. I do not have a prefabricated answer. The suffering I have seen and, at times, personally endured defies neatly configured definition. I can only tell you what I have discovered, what the Bible says, and trust that God will provide the necessary understanding.

It helps to realize that suffering was not part of God's original plan. There were no screams of pain, no mental impairments, no physical handicaps at creation. Neither is suffering allowed entrance into the heavenly world we one day will occupy. Suffering came with man's fall; and as long as the world and its inhabitants are in revolt against God, it must be dealt with. But our wrestling is against the backdrop of an all-powerful God who loved us enough to cast his only Son, Jesus Christ, into this caldron of trouble and woe. The Savior whom you call upon in distress is One who sympathizes with your agony and hurt, for he himself has suffered.

In this context, we recognize that suffering is inevitable but not permanent. And since our omnipotent God is truly all-loving, then even the horror and anguish of suffering must have an eventual design of good. Glance at the cross and see the blood, the jeers, the abandonment. How could God allow such a calamity? But where would we be apart from such an excruciating crucifixion? There would be no resurrection, no salvation, no hope of heaven. God, while not causing evil, does sovereignly allow it. It is never outside of his control or beyond his power to use it for good. We can actually glorify God when we respond rightly to suffering, and this itself should tell us that we can advance in our adversity.

Suffering refines our faith. The trivial is excised, the essential emphasized. Do we believe God in the face of it all? If so, we will grow and be strengthened. Suffering prepares us to comfort others. Words from smiling, indifferent faces to wounded hearts mean little; but words from a fellow sufferer support and uplift. Suffering removes artificial props of security and resets the stage of our personal world with new dependence on Christ. We cannot change the circumstance. We must trust God. As Jesus entrusted himself to the Father on the torture-rack of the cross, so we too entrust ourselves to our Savior.

Suffering is real. Don't deny it, but don't succumb to it. There is an end to it. And the God of all love can bring meaning and purpose to the darkest hour. "The God of all grace, who called you to his eternal glory in Christ, after you have suffered a little while, will himself restore you and make you strong, firm and steadfast" (1 Peter 5:10). This is God's promise to you.

There have been times in my life when I've questioned my suffering, when I've pled, "Why, Lord?" and not received a reply. Because of your sovereignty, you've allowed me an explanation for some of my sorrows, proving your protection toward me, and you have withheld explanations I may not be ready for. The hurt is real, but you can be the only comfort to me during those trying times. Though you did not author suffering, you can turn it around, giving it new meaning and purpose. And I thank you for it.

TOUCHSTONE

*Suffering is profitable when
we make the right
response.*

But the greatest of these is love.

1 Corinthians 13:13

Love Is ...

The greatest thing in the world is love. Nothing rivals its power to heal, restore, mend, and make all things new. Love surpasses all other virtues. Set into Scripture like a crown jewel, the thirteenth chapter of First Corinthians shimmers with the practical purity of love.

Love is "patient." It is never in a rush, never forceful, never demanding. It waits for God's best, whenever and whatever that may be. It refuses to yield to panic or grasp at temporal solutions.

Love is "kind." It acts in the best interest of others. It overlooks offenses. It is extravagant, giving more than what is asked or needed. Love "does not envy, it does not boast, it is not proud." It waits for God to promote and exalt. It credits him for the success and acknowledges the contributions of others. It applauds the gain of another. It does not flaunt or taunt, but bends its knee in humility.

Love is not "rude." It is polite and courteous to all, even to those who are ill-mannered or ill-tempered. Love is not "self-seeking." It does not relentlessly pursue personal perfection, but gives priority to the kingdom of God.

Love "is not easily angered and keeps no record of wrongs." It is not irritated by the behavior of others. It refuses to judge, leaving that to God. It does not keep a mental record of offenses. Love does not delight in evil, but rejoices with the truth. It meets each day with cheer and a smile. It thinks upon good things and is happy in simple obedience to God.

Love "never fails." It lasts. It works for anyone in any circumstance. It sets you free. It is always the right thing to do. When you choose to love, you have chosen God's way.

Measure your love by these attributes. When provoked or tempted, review this chapter and think on its brilliance. Let its truth light your path. If you are overwhelmed by the enormity of love, choose one of its features and commit yourself to obedience. Continually turn it over in your mind and heart until it is woven into your spirit.

If you are to reflect such love, you must put away "childish ways" (v. 11). Your goal is maturity in Christ, and the old way of living and thinking is a hindrance. God has made you a new creature, and love is the main ingredient. Renew your mind daily with the principles of God's Word, so that your emotions, intellect, and will may be greenhouses for the love of God to flourish.

Thanks for giving me such a clear description of love and its power, Father. I want these qualities to be real in my life, but I know that only you can make that happen. When I walk in love, I am wonderfully free, and that is how you want me to be.

TOUCHSTONE

You are never more like God
than when you love.

Éxperience God's Touch...

...with help from the four popular devotional books in the A Touch of His... series, written by Charles Stanley. Each book contains 31 meditations on a particular theme by Dr. Stanley, along with a Scripture passage, a personal prayer and a "Touchstone," or personal application. In addition, each meditation is accompanied by beautiful, original photography by Dr. Stanley himself, which makes these books perfect for gift-giving as well as personal reading.

Each hardcover book is priced at $12.99, and all four books, as well as audio versions, are available at fine Christian bookstores everywhere.

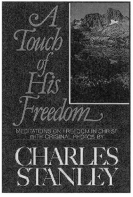

A Touch of His Freedom
0-310-54620-6

A Touch of His Wisdom
0-310-54540-4

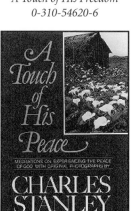

A Touch of His Peace
0-310-54550-1

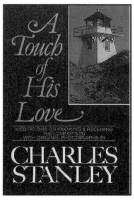

A Touch of His Love
0-310-54560-9